NAUTICAL JOBS HUNTER

First Steps towards a Hospitality Career at Sea or on Land

A POCKET BOOK

SÉRGIO CONSTANTINO

authorHOUSE®

AuthorHouse™ UK
1663 Liberty Drive
Bloomington, IN 47403 USA
www.authorhouse.co.uk
Phone: UK TFN: 0800 0148641 (Toll Free inside the UK)
*   UK Local: 02036 956322 (+44 20 3695 6322 from outside the UK)*

Published by AuthorHouse 03/24/2021

ISBN: 978-1-6655-8759-4 (sc)
ISBN: 978-1-6655-8758-7 (e)

Print information available on the last page.

How to prepare for a job with a cruise liner,
yacht, ferry, cargo ship and hotels

PREFACE

Cruise hips carry over 10 million passengers each year. Before the COVID-19 pandemic, a new cruise ship was launched almost every month. Although the cruise line business has gone down dramatically companies are building new ships to adapt to the situation, most at a rate of one or two cruise ships per year.

Cruise line companies employ more than 100,000 crew of all ages, backgrounds and nationalities—about fifty different nationalities from all over the world. The cruise industry has been the most rapidly expanding area of the leisure and travel industry, meeting the demand from passengers who long for a taste of the salt sea air, the luxury of life aboard majestic cruise ships that are floating five star hotels, and the excitement of sailing to sun-drenched paradises across the world. Sailing the oceans, all crew members have the opportunity to visit paradise all over the world, to meet new friends of all nationalities, and to travel for free and get paid well for it.

The yacht industry provides the higher salaries in these days. most of the yacht companies seek beautiful stewardesses to join their teams, and in my opinion they give more importance to beauty than to experience.The coming years will bring a lot of expedition ships which will sail to remote places in the Antarctica Peninsula, the Falkland Islands, Elephant sland, South Georgia, and other locations in parts of the globe they previously never visited this is a magical career opportunity for all who want to start new careers at sea and as well as the most experienced professionals.

This publication in pocket-book size is intended to provide first-step career information for those who want to initiate careers at sea, how to obtain the right certificates, courses, diplomas, and visas needed to work with such greatteams on board these beautiful ships. It is intendedto support the thousands of new candidates, professional crew members and o potential applicants who have neither the time nor the knowledge to research the steps one must go through to work in luxury ocean cruises, luxury yachts, ferry companies, cargo ships, and hotels all over the world. This book outlines each position and department and the steps for each course in obtaining the requisite certificates and diplomas.

This pocket book is the sequel to my *Nautical Jobs Hunter: Cruise Career Guide book 2007–2008*. he new *Nautical Jobs Hunter 2: Cruise Career Guide 2021* offers updated information with loads of new companies, agencies, agents, and concessionaires all over the world. It is aimed at helping everyone who is interested in working in the cruise industry, whether at sea or with the hotel industry ashore.

Working in ocean cruises, yachts, ferries, and hotels around the world has been the passion of my life. I first went to work on an ocean cruise in 1991, at the age of 21 Since then I have never stopped working in the industry. At 50 years of age, I have a very open mind. ormally at work I can support all the departments: I can work as a manager, as a kitchen orter, as a steward or in any department, and this is brilliant. ll of us should be able to support and help others on any occasion, any time. In the course of a lifetime, the learning never, never stops, we are learning every single day, every moment in our lives. I am still working, and I will be the rest of my days, because for me hospitality is magical so much to give, so much to learn, to teach, to help and support others.

I would like to thank all the naval schools which provide the courses needed to work at sea and have confirmed for me the courses each candidate must take in the present day. We have taken care to authenticate all the material mentioned, and it has been checked whenever possible as well with shipping companies, publications. While we cannot be held responsible for errors or omissions, o the best of our knowledge all the information is correct and up-to-date at the time of publication.

SERGIO CONSTANTINO

INTRODUCTION

A cruise ship in many aspects is like a floating luxury resort, providing numerous opportunities and career choices comparable to those of the resort leisure industry.

There is free accommodation (usually shared with someone in the same profession), good food, the pleasure of travelling to exotic countries, and making new friends as you learn about new traditions and customs from many different countries. It is a great way to save money and see the world.

A high standard of service and a well-groomed uniform is expected from all staff and crew members. The hours are long, and the work is hard, though it will become easier to do after a time. t the cruise lines, you will be expected to worktwelve hours a day, sometimes more. But while working in this industry can be hard with long hours, it can be very rewarding in so many ways. Good salaries are paid and in most cases are tax free. ips and commissions are usually very good.

There are unlimited opportunities for employment on board, but you must have the ability to do the job applied for and be well trained or willing to be trained for a position that best suits your own talents, skills, and experience.

If you have the right qualifications, it will be much easier to apply for any position you would like to apply for, and you will have many more opportunities to join any company because of the constant turnover in staff. Turnover results from contracts endings, crew going on holidays or being moved to another ship of the company, the addition of new ships, and the dismissal of crew members. Most new crew members move on in their careers, get promoted, or stay only for short contracts, all of which contributes to an enormous turnover in staff.

You must realize that getting a job is not easy: you have to be positive, persistent, and very much sought-after because of the attraction of travelling and the rewards the cruise ship industry brings. This results in many applicants being sent to cruise, yacht, and ferry companies. ou must therefore prepare an excellent CV or résumé with your work history and a letter of application.When you apply to a company, take care and make sure you have a current passport, a C-1/D visa or a Schengen visa, STCW 10 Manila Basic Safety Training certificate, a ro-ro passenger safety course, the appropriate afety wareness course, and any others required for each position in the hotel or marine departments.

CHAPTER 1

MAKING CONTACT AND PREPARING FOR SUCCESS

The first step in considering what kind of job you are suited for is to contact as many employers as you can, either directly through the career opportunities link on the companies' websites or through their agencies and agents around the world, which post opportunities on their websites. Make sure you don't pay to work in the cruise industry, as legitimate companies will never ask you to pay anything, except possibly fo flights if they aren't covered in your contract. If any agency or agent asks you to pay any fee so that you can join a company, don't pay, these are scams.

My previous book *Nautical* (2007) and the updated book you're currently reading (both available on the website of the publisher, www.authorhouse.co.uk) will provide you with loads of contacts from major companies and some of the finest hotels around the world, including phone numbers, fax numbers, emails, descriptions of each job available, departments information, and itinerarie all a great help when you are looking for a job at sea.The more you contact, the better chance you have of being accepted, so apply to as many cruise lines, yachts, ferry companies, agencies a agents as possible

Having certained the name and address of the company you are applying to, present your application letter, which should be short and written neatly or typed professionally, together with your CV or résumé listing your work history, skills, . A full-length picture is worth a thousand words, Include your full name, address, phone number, email, and position applied for. Also enclose photocopies of references, certificates, and diplomas. remember, cruise companies and hotels reserve hundreds of letters of applications, so if you have well-presented application materials, your chances of getting an interview are much higher.

If you post your cv/application materials, use a large envelope so that everything will arrive flat and neat, not folded. A presentation in a folder is also useful.cruise companies have worldwide offices, so many nationalities can apply.

Be sure to sell yourself: include any special skills and languages. t is essential to address your application to the appropriate department, preferably using the name of the relevant person in charge of recruiting for the job you are applying for or sending it to the Director of Human Resources. Using a name will make a better impression than one addressed to *Dear Sir or Madam.*

Occasionally contracts are offered solely on the quality of your application. We have spoken to staff who had been interviewed by telephone and emails and then offered a contract because of the professionalism they demonstrated in the application process.

Once again, I advise you never to pay a fee to work. f an agency or agent asks you to pay a fee, refuse, a scam companies and legitimate agencies or agents will never ask you to pay any fee, though this scheme is becoming more and more popular t can be very discouraging as well and disheartening if some companies don't even bother to reply you, and while this happens in many cases, never give up, keep making contact and applying.

If you do not hear from a cruise company within 8 weeks resubmit your application or send a update of your cv, do not telephone unless if is absolutely necessary, most personnel departments strongly discourage telephone enquiries as they are notoriously busy.

If you do telephone, announce your name clearly in a friendly tone of voice, clearly state which department you wish to speak to help to make the best impression of yourself, we have included in the pocket book initial career steps, many useful hints, suggestions and guidelines on how to apply and what positions are available together with each certificates, courses, diplomas you need to take so that you can apply for your dream job, this information has been put together with the assistance of many of the major cruise companies, yachts and ferry companies, also agents, agencies to ensure the accuracy of the material contained within the book.

Example of letter of application

Date: 21/01/2021 Philip Morris
Mr. john Foster Central Drive
Director of Human Resources RG24 8FY
Royal Caribbean Cruise Line Chineman
Miami/Florida/USA United Kingdom

Dear Mr. Foster

I am writing you to apply for a position in on of the Retail shops on your cruise ships.

I am 35 years of age and have been employed for the past three years as a Sale Assistant in a large up market department store.

I feel that my experience to date would make me a useful member of your crew and I am well motivated to take my career in this direction.

I enjoy working with the public and dealing with problems and therefore this, along with my willingness to learn and organizational skills would make me a good candidate for the job.

I can make myself full available for interview at your convenience.

I enclose my cv, photograph and references and as well my certificates and thank you for taking the time to consider my application.

I look forward to hear from you.

Yours sincerely.
Philip Morris

Interview Guidelines

- Be punctual, go for your interview alone.
- Be smartly dressed, do not wear jeans, to much jeweler, strong perfume, aftershave or have outrageous hairstyles.
- Presentation is very important.
- First impression are very significant, many of jobs as been lost by not adhering the above instructions.
- Be informed, find out everything you can about the company structure, ships in the fleet and itineraries.
- Ensure you known how the interviewer name is pronounced.
- Be alert, tactful, sincere and courteous, show interest and enthusiasm and most importantly ask questions about the company and the job, that will impress the interviewer.

Be prepared to answer standard questions, e.g

- What qualifications do you have?
- What are your qualities?
- What are your present duties/responsibilities?
- Why do you want this particularly job?
- What other companies have you approached?
- Why did you apply for this particularly company?
- Present a positive picture, greet the interviewer in a confident manner, do not smoke, even if invited by the employer, smile often.

- If you don't understand a question, ask for clarification.
- Do not criticize former employers.
- Establish your personal strengths, skills, experience and qualifications.
- –Carry out a copy your CV/References, Certificates, Diplomas with you and make sure you have a 10 years passport.
- Ask questions about the job, hours, salary, length of contract, promotions prospects and of course about the company.
- Do not give impression that you are only interested in cruising the world and seeing exotic places.
- The position you are applying for it is the most important aspect of your interview.
- Always remember, cruise companies will hire the best person available for the job, if you do not have all the skills required you can still be chose for the job and be trained in areas you are not competent in or you may be offered a alternative position.
- Be positive with your answers.
- First impressions are lasting ones.
- Even if a company states it might be able to offer you a job, it could be months before you are called for a interview.
- In some cases companies offer positions up to 1 year after a application as been submitted because someone as let them down, successful applicants often drop out for one reason or another, so it is important to make sure that your details are kept on file by updating them every so often.

- You may be contacted urgently, so be always prepared.

Be prepared for rejection

- If you get a interview but are not offered a job, don't take it personally, the person who did get the job may have been better qualified, more experienced or have given offer better answers than you in that day.
- Phone or write to the person who interviewed you thanking them for them time and the advice and ask if there will be a vacancy soon, it shows you are enthusiastic to work for the company and as they have already meet you, they may just offer the next job for you.
- If not, you might find out why you did not get the job and rectify the problem for the future.
- Keep applying.
- Make use of what you have learned.
- Call and ask for your details to be kept on file.
- Call and ask if there are any similar jobs you could be consider for.
- Apply for the same job again after a few months later.
- Look over your CV, does he need improving?
- Have you had enough land based experience? If not delay your application until you get.
- Reflect areas of improvement.
- Call and ask for feedback after a interview.
- Find out details of the history of the company.

Courses needed by position

CAPTAIN

Seaman' s book, Medical Certificate, STCW A-11/2 o A-III/2, STCW A-V/2, STCWA-VI/1-1-2-3-4, Advanced C.I (STCW _A-VI/3), Survival, Fast rescue boats (STCW A-VI/2-1), Fast Rescue boats (STCW A-VI/2-2), GMDSS (STCW A-VI/2), ARPA (STCW 8-I/1-2), Ecdis (STCW A-II/1.2.3 and Order FOM 2472/2006, ISPS (A-VI/5), Advanced Sanitary Formation (STCW A-VI/4-2 (FORMAC III)

STAFF CAPTAIN – (same as Captain)

1 ST Officer –Seaman's Book, Maritime medical certificate, Officials (STCW a-II/2 or A-III/2); Ro Ro Passenger Safety certificate (STCW A-V/2); STCW A-V/6 (Basic formation of Protection; Basic Safety (STCW-A-VI/1-1-2-3-4); Advanced C.I (STCW A-VI/3); Emb. Survival, Fast rescue boats (STCW a-VI/2-1); Fast Rescue boats (STCW A-VI /2-2); GMDSS (STCW A-IV/2); ARPA (STCW B-1/12); ECDIS (STCW A-II/1-2-3 and Orden FOM 2472/2006); Advanced Sanitary Formation (STCW A-VI/4-2)FORMAC III;

2nd OFFICER and 3rd OFFICER –Seaman's Book; Maritime Medical Certificate; OFFICIALS (STCW A II/1 or A-III/1); Ro Ro passenger safety (STCW A-V/2); Basic Protection Formation (STCW A-VI-6); Basic Protection (STCW A-VI/1-2-3-4); Advanced C.I (STCW A-VI/3); Survival embarkation and Rescue Fast Boats (STCW A-VI/2-1); GMDSS (STCW A-VI/2); ARPA (STCW B-1/12); ECDIS (STCW A-II/1-2-3 and ORDEN FOM

2472/2006); Advanced Sanitary Formation (STCW A-VI/4-2 (FORMAC III)

CHIEF Engineer and 1ˢᵗ Engineer Officer – Seaman's Book, Maritime Medical Certificate, Officials (STCW A-II/2 or A-III/2); Ro Ro passenger safety certificate (STCW A-V/2); Formation in Basic Protection (STCWA-VI/6); Basic Formation (STCW A-VI/1-1-2-3-4); Advanced CI (STCW A-VI/3); Survival Embarkations, Fast Rescue Boats (STCWA-VI/2-1); Initial Sanitary Formation (STCW –A-VI/4-1) FORMAC II);

2ⁿᵈ Engineer Officer – Seaman's Book, Maritime Medical Certificate; Officials (STCW A-II/1 or A-III/1); Ro Ro Passenger safety certificate (STCW A-VI/6); Formation in Basic Protection (STCW A VI/6); Basic Formation (STCW A-VI/1-1-2-3-4); Advanced CI (STCW A VI/3); Survival embarkations and Fast Rescue Boats (STCW A-VI/2-2); Initial Sanitary Formation (STCW A-VI/4-2 (FORMAC III)

COUNTERMASTER / Deckland 1-2-3-4-5-6 – Seaman's Book, Maritime Medical Certificate; Bridge Seaman (STCW A-II/4); Ro Ro passenger safety (STCW A-V/2); Formation in Basic Protection (STCW A-VI/6); Basic Formation (STCW A-VI/1-1-2-3-4); Survival Embarkation and Fast Rescue Boats (STCW A-VI/2-1); Fast Rescue Boat STCW A-VI/2-2 only Deckland 4)

Machine Sailor nr 1-2 (Seaman's Book, Maritime Medical Certificate; Machine Sailor certificate (STCW A-III/4); Ro Ro passenger safety certificate (STCW A-V/2); Basic

Protection Formation (STCW A-VI/6); Basic Formation (STCW A-VI/1-1-2-3-4); Survival Embarkations and Fast Rescue Boats (STCW A-VI/2-2); Machine Sailor 2 as to take Fast Rescue Boats (STCW A-VI/2-2)

FOR ALL THE HOTEL (RESTAURANT/BAR/ KITCHEN/HOUSEKEEPING), ENTERTAINMENT, GIFT SHOPS AND OTHER POSITIONS EVERY ONE AS TO TAKE FIRST THE STCW10 MANILLA CERTIFICATE OF BASIC SAFETY STCW A-VI/6, BASIC FORMATION (STCW A-VI/1.1.2.3.4), SURVIVAL EMBARKATION AND RESCUE FAST BOATS (STCW A-VI/2-2), CROWD MANAGEMENT CERTIFICATE, SAFETY AWARENESS CERTIFICATE for the HOTEL DEPARTMENT, GET THE MARITIME MEDICAL CERTIFICATE AND THAN REQUEST WITH THIS ONES THE SEAMAN'S BOOK.

DOCTOR / NURSES

STCW (Survival at sea, Fire Prevention and Fire Fighting, First Aid; Social Responsibilities onboard); Security Awareness Training / Security Awareness Training for all seafarers' with designated security duties; Crowd Management and Safety Training for Personnel Providing Direct Service to Passengers in Passenger spaces Course; Crisis Management and Human Behavior Course; Passenger Ship Course; Survival Embarkation and Rescue Boats (STCW A-VI/2-2)

ALSO NEEDS TO TAKE THE RO RO PASSENGER SAFETY CERTIFICATE, SAFETY AWARENESS CERTIFICATE,

Have a passport on date for 10 years, if you will be requested to join a ship in USA the companies will give you the C1D visa, if you will join in Europe you must have a SCHENGEN VISA.

NOTE: Bridge and Machine Sailors which not participate in a watch keeping –STCW A-VI . 1.1.2.3.4, Electric officer: A-III/6 – Electronic sailor : A-III/7

Advanced CI for all personal which will be in control for all operations.

Advanced Sanitary Formation only for Captains and Officers in guard of navigation.

Rescue boats not fast – Raft Chef and Raft Patterns

Searching for jobs at sea

When you are ready with the courses and certificates it will be the time to start to send your applications to and all you want and need to send, as much as you send at the sometime, more probably you will get the chance to be invited for a interview.

You can find all the courses you need to take in any NAVAL School across your own country, you must contact the schools and check with them in which dates they have available the courses to start, normally the schools waits that they have at least 10 students to make the courses, normally this schools are near the coast of each country but they can be find as well in the center of your country, you should search for the schools online and check which ones are better for you to make your courses, the prices are more or less the same all over, but you can find cheaper ones in other countries, the thing is, you should study how much you will spend doing the course at your own country and how much you will spend doing the courses in another country with the travel expenses.

You can find positions available in every website of each single company, they have a area for careers and you can apply directly with the companies.

In them websites you can find as well information about all the agents and agencies they work all across the world and also they advise you about SCAMS online, be careful when you are applying, once again, NEVER PAY ANY FEE TO WORK.

Ask the following questions at your interview

1. Length of Contract
   How long is it for? Is the contract subject to the successful completion of a probationary work period? If you are permanent (i.e. career posts such as officers and engineering staff) contracts as no limit, however most of the crew are hired on a contractual basis, almost every company in the cruise industry including agents and concessionaires provide contracts prior to start to work.

They usually fair and responsible and generally renewed each time you return from leave, always read the small print and ask questions before signing.

2. Commission (If interviewed by a agent/concessionaire)
    Will you pay commission to them on your earnings? If so, for how long?
    Some agents/concessionaires demand commission on follow up contracts or additional offers of employment even although you have obtained it independently, I recommend you to get a position directly with the web site of the companies and them platforms, they will not charge you nothing, as the agencies and agents receive very good commissions from every one they put to work on the ships and finish them contracts, the ones which are demanding you to pay commissions they are only taking money from the 2 sides.

3. Medical
    Always check whether or not you will be provided with insurance and medical coverage for illness, injury, etc, find out if they are any exclusions, check exactly what you are covered for, as you may have to take out a personal insurance policy.

4. Salary
    Salaries are usually paid every week on ocean cruises, monthly on yachts and ferry boats, you can have your salary to be transferred to your bank account in your home country, you can also bank this at the Pursers Office, if a concessionaire employs you that company pays you separately, tax is usually not deducted if you

are out of the country for over six months and have a contract for one year, check this with your local tax office.

5. Taxation
Will your earnings be subject to tax deductions, if so will it be deducted from your salary by your employer?

6. Travel
Ask who will pay your travel expenses to and from the embarkation port, if your future employer is going or not going to part or fully pay, will they reimburse you on successful complete ion of your contract, the later is the policy of many of the cruise companies.

7. Uniforms
Are uniforms provided free of charge? If no where do you get them? Some companies provide you uniform for free, others they charge you after, usually working uniforms are supplied and cleaned, in most cases for service personnel, uniform jackets only are considered working uniform and are cleaned/laundered at the company expenses, most service personnel will require to purchase, company approved black pants, white shirts, bow ties, cummerbunds, black shoes and will be responsible to clean/launder brushes.

If you are told that your contract will not be available until you board ship you must obtain a letter of appointment from your future employer stating the name of the ship you will be joining and the date of commencement of your job, this is very necessary as you are required to produce this for the immigration authorities when entering the country where you will be pick up the ship, you also require this to get your Seaman's Book, you may also require vaccination certificates but ask that question at your interview.

CONTRACT OF EMPLOYMENT

OCEAN CRUISES

This is to certify that:
Name of Applicant)

Holder Passport Nr:

Has a confirmed position on board the:
(Name of the Vessel)

Country of Registry:

To serve in the position of:

Applicant to report on or about:

At the U.S.A port in:
NON-U.S.A port(s) at which this vessel normally includes)

Please issue this person a C1D Visa and D Visa or Schangen Visa

If the above named seaman is granted a transit visa for his purpose and fails to join the vessel to which he is destined within the period of time for which he is admitted, this company will be responsible for any costs incurred in deporting him to his home country or to the country which he as obtained his transit visa.

Signed:

Authorized company official
Ocean Cruises

GUIDELINES

Physical examination for the most major cruise liners nd/or their concessionaires include.

1. Measurement of height, weight, blood pressure, temperature, pulse and respiration.
2. Titmus vision testing and near, far and color vision.
3. Audimetric screnning (ANSI-69 reference levels) from 500Hz to 600Hz

Examination by a physician to include, but not limited to:

A. Funduscopic examination
B. Examination of tympanic membranes
C. Evaluation of tyroid size and search for presence of cervical adenopathy.
D. Chest Auscultation.

E. Heart evaluation to include auscultation for murmuts or arrhythmias and estimation of heart size.

F. Abdominal examination for presence for masses or enlarged organs.

G. Check the hernia, varicocles, hydrococles or testicular masses on all males.

H. Examination of stool for occult blood in all patients over 45 years of age.

I. Evaluation of range of joint motion and spinal alignment in both males and females.

J. Basic muscle strength testing on deck crew employees.

K. Neurologic evaluation.

L. Examination of skin for rashes or pathological lesions.

M. Lymphatic system evaluation for evidence of enlarged lymph nodes

Other examination and / or testing may be included depending upon findings on initial encounter.

RULES AND REGULATIONS

Whatever your rank is, you will be require to obey the rules and regulations of the ship, e.g. time keeping conduct and appearance.

Several areas of the ship will be out of bounds depending on your position and permission to socialize with passengers may not be allowed, in most of the ships there is a curfew system whereby all of duty members of staff other than senior officers must vacate the passenger areas when require.

Crew members breaking rules will be given written or verbal warnings, this ones can be 1 way out of the company, they can be 1 single warning or 3 written /verbal depending on situations and why if anyone will continue to get warnings they will be dismissed.

Other areas for instant dismissal are missing the ship, drunk people, taking drugs, fighting or swearing in the passenger areas and use of naked flame in your accommodation areas.

ACCOMMODATION

Staff accommodation on a cruise ships, yacht or ferry depends on your particular job and the ship you are working on, Officers and Senior Employees usually have passenger cabins in different areas of the ship which are difficult to sell, staff accommodation is usually shared by 2 or 4, depending of the ship, normally everyone get a shared cabin with someone.

Crew accommodation on the new ships are of a very high standard.

FOOD&BEVERAGE

Larger ships may have staff restaurants for different nationalities with waiter service while smaller ships reserve a section of the passenger restaurant for staff sometimes, depending on the ship, Officers are usually permitted to eat at the passenger buffet and in certain evenings, most ships also have a crew bar and recreation area and on some of bigger ships their own gymnasium, sub bathing areas and splash pool.

CREW SHOPS

The majority of the ships have a crew shop where you can buy items such as soup, toothpaste, shampoo, cigarettes, etc, if there is no crew shop you may be allowed to buy from the passenger shops at certain times of the day with a great discount.

MAILING AND TELEPHONE HOME

Mail from home is sent to you through your company Head Office, it is than forwarded to the ship via Port agents or alternatively it can be sent directly to the Port of Agents (the purser will supply you with a list of names and addresses), every ship as a international recognized call sign, if you wish to receive a call while you are at sea, give the caller the name of the ship and its call sign, this can be obtained from the Cruise Line Company, if you wish to phone someone you are better waiting until you go ashore and use the phones at the dock side, it will be much less expensive than calling from the ship.

DOCUMENTATION

You will require a full 10 year Passport together with a Seaman's Visa (C1D Visa or Shangen Visa), this are available on the embassies and it is valid for 5 years, before contacting your Embassy you will require to supply written proof of offer employment e.g. contract of employment or letter of appointment.

GOING ASHORE

When you board the ship you will receive a crew ID card, your pass will be placed in a box at the entrance of the ship with a number relating your crew number, this enables the Crew Purser to see who is on board or out, it is taken with you when you leave the ship ashore and you most put back when you get back.

VISA and WORK PERMITS

Most employees do not require a work permit or visa since most of the ships are registered in countries with non restrictive employment laws, employees however must have a full Passport if you are sailing to or on from American ports and you are not a US citizen you will also require a Visa (C1D visa), this is obtained from US embassies and is issued on receipt of a offer of employment or a actual contract.

If a Visa is require whilst on board the ship to visit any country which requires one, it will be arranged by your Crew Purser, additionally please check if you are visiting any countries which require vaccination certificates.

FINANCIAL MATTERS

Some cruise companies, yachts and ferry companies will pay your travel expenses to join the ship, but many will make the crew pay at least in the first instance, in some cases they will pay a percentage of the flight cost and reimburse travelling expenses at a later date, make sure this is specified in your contract.

Salaries will be payee in different ways, they can be

payee on board by the Crew Purser in hand or they can be payee through bank account transfer.

PREPARATION TO JOIN A SHIP(NECESSARY DOCUMENTS)

- Letter of employment and contract.
- Passport
- Driving license (if you have one)
- Letter from your doctor about any medication necessary as this may not be always available on board, carry sufficient with you.
- Return Air ticket
- Insurance certificate if necessary
- Copy of your birth certificate
- Currency of the country you will be joining the ship in, as your ship may arrive later than the estimated time due the weather, etc and this also tide over until you get your first salary.
- Major credit card (if you have) for emergencies.
- C-1D Visa
- Seaman's Record Book
- STCW10 Manilla or other on date
- Crowd Management certificate
- Safety Awareness certificate
- Ro Ro Passenger safety certificate (Ferries)
- International certificate of inoculations and vaccinations (against yellow fever)

PACKING

You should bear in the mind that you probably have small cabin space, so just take essential items.

EMBARKATION

When you arrive at the port of embarkation, you will expected to report to the cruise/yacht/ferry company or agent's office to confirm your arrival, this must be done during office hours, if it is not possible, call first thing in the morning the following day, but the company should give you a 24 hours phone number so that you can call and inform them, details of this should be included in your letter of appointment, remember to take your contract of employment or letter of appointment with you or both, as this will be required by immigration, the cruise company or agent will help you if you have any problem with this.

SELECTING YOUR JOB

Before going any further, this is the point where you must decide which job you are best qualified to do aboard the ship, only apply for a position that you are confident, that you can undertake.

POSITIONS AVAILABLE

LISTED BELOW ARE MOST OF THE POSITIONS AVAILABLE ON A CRUISE SHIP, YACHT, FERRY BOAT, CARGO SHIP, HOTEL

BARS

Bar Manager; Assistant Bar Supervisor; Assistant Bar Manager; Bar Supervisor; Bar Boy, Bar utility

BEAUTY/FITNESS

Aerobic instructor; Fitness instructor, Salon Manager; Assistant Salon Manager; Beauticians, Cosmetologists; Hair Stylists; Massage Therapists; Nail Technicians

DECK DEPARTMENT

Captain; Staff Captain; Chief Officer; 1st Officer; 2nd Officer, 3rd Officer, Radio Officer, Security Officer, Safety Officer; Quartermaster, Bosun, Able Seaman, Carpenter, Deck utility Man, Painter

ENGINEERING DEPARTMENT

Chief engineer, 1st Engineer, 2nd Engineer, 3rd engineer, Junior engineer, Engine Storekeeper, Engine Repairman, Chief Electrician, Chief Electrician Tech, Electronic technician, Air condition tech, Deck Engine Mech, Engine cadet, Plumber.

GALLEY/KITCHEN

Executive Chef, Assistant Executive chef, Sous Chef, Chef Tourant, Chef de Partie, 1st Cook, Cook Trainee, Crew Cook, Assistant Crew Cook, Commis Chef, Crew Cook

Utility, Cooks runner, Storekeeper, Provision Master, Pastry Chef, Butcher, Baker, Buffet Man

RETAIL STAFF

Gift Shop Manager, Assistant Gift Shop Manager, Gif Shop Assistant

MEDICAL

Doctor, Physiotherapist, Nurse

CRUISE/ENTERTAINMENT STAFF

Cruise Director, Assistant Cruise Director, Social Host/Hostess, Assistant Cruise Staff, Port Lecture, Art Auctioneer, Shore Excursion Manager, Assistant Shore Excursion Manager, Administration Child Care, Cruise Staff Steward, Gentleman Host, Entertainer, Choreographer, Disc Jockey, Production Manager, State Manager, Sound/Light Technician, Video Technician, Videographer, Television Technician, Guest Speakers, Instructors, Specialist Acts.

HOTEL STAFF

Hotel Manager, Chief Purser, Hotel Purser, Crew Purser, Assistant Purser, PA/Secretary, Junior Assistant Purser, Hotel Assistant, Guest Service Co-or, Front Desk Assistants, Programmer Coordinator, Information Officer, Guest Relation Officer, Journalist/Writer, Accountant, Assistant Accountant, IT Staff, Air/Sea Agent.

HOUSEKEPPING

Housekeeper, Supervisor, Head Cabin Steward(ess), Cabin Steward/Stewardess, Butler, Bell Captain, Pool Attendant, Laundry Keeper, Linen Keeper and Assistants.

RESTAURANT STAFF

Maitre D' Hotel, F&B Manager, Assistant F&B Manager, Restaurant Manager, Assistant Restaurant Manager, Head Waiter/Waitress, Waiter/Waitress, Wine Steward/Stewardess, Busboy (Runner)

PHOTOGRAPHERS - Photo Manager, Photographer.

JOB DESCRIPTIONS

THE BRIGDE

THE CAPTAIN

The Captain is in charge of the entire ship, maritime laws a inheritance from the ancients, gives the Captain total dictatorial rights over the ship and all who sail with him, passengers, officers and crew, as well as over seeing the navigation, the Captain's daily routine is largely taken up0 with paper works, inspection tours, attending social events and meeting with the various head of departments.

A Captain paper work alone will be sufficient to drive a ordinary mortal over the brink, everything by law must be filed and recorded, the ship's log include reports from every major department including daily statements from the ship's medical department regarding drugs issued, alcohol, passengers treated and their progress, the Captain except in the event of illness or absence when the Staff Captain assumes command is the only officer entitled to touch the log, he must file endless details of weather, navigation factors, distance travelled, fuel consumed and engineering reports and schedules, he is everything from navigational wizard to charming dinner companion, from fire Chief to Master of Ceremonies, he has to deal

With many different nationalities, sometime upwards of fifty, a true overall genius at all times.

STAFF CAPTAIN

The Staff Captain is second in command, he is fully qualified and trained in his own right and draws a salary not far behind on the Captain, he is in charge of the ship when the Captain is on vacation or off ill.

The two men generally divide duties according to individual interests, for example if the Captain is happiest with is charts and seafaring duties, much of the entertainment obligation may be passed to the Staff Captain, he is in charge of the deck department, he overseas all aspects of safety and security issues of the ship, its passengers and crew, investigates accidents, incidents and non conformities.

CHIEF OFFICER

He is responsible for the external cleanliness, care and maintenance of the hull, superstructure, rig, cargo gear, mooring equipment, gangways and ladders as well as safety equipment, assists the Staff Captain with interior maintenance program me for the deck and refurbishing in cooperation with the Hotel Manager, administers the maintenance program me for the deck and refurbishing related issues to Hotel, assists the Staff Captain with the budget, co operates with the Safety Officer and Security Officer in accident/incident reporting instructs and trains crewmembers in general seamen ship and in matters concerning safety, security and protection for the environment, prepares stability calculations.

FIRST OFFICER

The First Officer is a watch keeping officer in charge of a navigational watch, he is also assigned some of the following tasks, keeping maintenance records for all navigational equipment, corrections to chats, pilor books, light lists and other nautical publications, maintenance of all navigational lights, proper storage of signals, rockets or other emergency signaling equipment, supervises the maintenance of ship's lifeboats, rescue boats and tenders, supervision of inspections and maintenance of the ship's portable firefighting equipment.

SECOND OFFICER

The Second Officer is a watch keeping officer in charge of a navigational watch or assisting a First Officer during such a watch, he /she is also assigned some of the following tasks, keeps maintenance records for all navigational equipment, corrections to charts, pilot books, light lists and other emergency signaling equipment, supervises the maintenance of the ship's portable firefighting equipment, ensures operation and inspection of watertight doors, supervises testing of fire screen doors, he/she trains the crew in safety in conjunction with safety, security and other marine officers.

CHIEF RADIO / COMMUNICATION OFFICER

He is in charge of onboard communications, he/she ensures that all radio communications are in accordance with applicable national and international regulations, assists the Master in ensuring all ship's certificates are accurate and current, maintain radio logbook and radio accounts, maintains the emergency radio equipment onboard and in the lifeboats supervises and trains crew in the operation of this equipment, updates database regarding marine officers and crew qualifications and licenses.

TRAINING OFFICER

He/ She reports to the Staff Captain, plans, coordinates and overseas training, delivers certain training as determined by the company, drives employee activity programmers, determines training needs, compiles data and analyses past and current year training equipments and interfaces the training requirements, schedules training for assigned instructors and supervisory personnel in effective techniques of training such as new employees, orientation, on job training, health and safety practices, etc.

CHIEF ENGINEER

The responsibility of a Chief Engineer is endless, ventilation, engine, refrigeration, air conditioning, the electrical system and plumbing, every nut, bolt and the door handle also falls under his domain.

The Chief Engineer's office as a computer centre which is a duplicate of the control panel on the bridge, there is a bank of dials that monitor every pulse beat of the diesels and check water pressure, machines that convert seawater into drinking water, below the Chief Engineer are the Second, Third and Fourth Engineers at appropriate areas of their training and careers.

CHIEF ENGINEER JNR

The Chief Engineer jnr is the deputy and second in command of the engine department, should be familiar with the Chief Engineer duties and assists the Chief Engineer in all service matters, co ordinates the repair and maintenance, is responsible for the repair and maintenance work in the engine rooms and the Hotel Department, assists with the budget.

FIRST ENGINEER

The First Engineer is the responsible leader for all work that as been carried out in the engine room and for the training of new engine crewmembers, responsible for bunkering, deck crames, mooring and anchor winches, transfer of oil and sludge, sewage and laundry drain tanks with attached equipment, sewage treatment plans, sewage pumps and ejectors, firefighting equipment, safety equipment, fire pumps, workshops, including tools and equipment, chain blocks and cranes in the engine room.

SECOND ENGINEER

The Second Engineer is a watch keeping Engineer, in addition to watch duties the position is assigned various maintenance and repair duties in the engine room

THIRD ENGINEER

The Third Engineer is responsible for the maintenance and repair of engines and related systems/equipment.

CHIEF ELECTRICIAN

The Chief Electrician is responsible to the Chief Engineer for the operation and maintenance of the electrical plant and associated systems in accordance with applicable regulation, he also assists with training of Assistant Electricians in safety procedures, assigned duties and assists the Chief Engineer with the department's budget.

FIRST ELECTRICIAN

The First Electrician in conjunction with the Chief Electrician is responsible for the operation and maintenance of the electrical plant and associated systems in accordance with the applicable regulation, he also assists with training of Assistant Electricians in safety procedures, assigned duties and assists the Chief Engineer with the department budget.

REFRIGERATION ENGINEER

Responsible for the operation and maintenance of the ventilation provision and air conditioning plant, co ordination and control of the refrigeration budget, training of Assistant Refrigeration Engineer in procedures and duties.

ASSISTANT REFRIGERATION ENGINEER

Reporting to the Refrigeration Engineer, maintenance and repair of the ventilation and provision of air conditioning plant as determined by the Refrigeration Engineer.

CHIEF SECURITY OFFICER

A Chief Security Officer is responsible for the prevention and detection of crime and maintenance of law order onboard the ship, he/ She advises the Captain of any incidents that have occurred or that are likely to occur, ensures that the rules and regulations are not breached by passenger or crew, acts as prosecutor at the Captain's court and as to be able to advise on points of law procedure.

He She puts in place security measures at the gangway when docked and should be aware of the current protocol and procedures in relation to local customs and immigration regulations and ensure none are breached, this is when the ship is more vulnerable, ensures that only visitors or officials board the ship` by means of pass, he/ she investigates minor and serious crime, therefore must have experience in the field of drug use, advises the Captain of any intelligence reports received as to threat assessments in any particular port or location, as to be mindful with effect act of terrorism would have on the ships.

The Security Officer should have experience in bomb search techniques and provide training by means of regular drills onboard the vessel.

He/ she as to be able to act rationally in demanding situations, should there be a fire or similar threat onboard the ship, prevent store ways from boarding the ship and have a idea if international migration law and handling procedures, if stowaways are caught, ensures the hull of the ship (The Shell) is watertight and that all hatches are properly battened down, investigates in conjunction with the ship's Doctor, all incidents to ensure false insurance claims are not made against the ship.

TRADESMEN

Every ships require 24 hours a day maintenance staff of all descriptions including carpenters, plumbers', electricians, etc, salaries differ from cruise company to cruise company but will be according to age and experience, it is normally the on shore trade rate, he reports to the Head of Engineering, the salaries given are very approximate and for the guidance only.

We must steed that the salaries and conditions vary greatly companies.

HOTEL DEPARTMENT

Position in Hotel Department

Hotel Director; Hotel Controller; Assistant Hotel Manager; Chief Purser; Crew Purser; Auditor; Assistant

Purser; 1st, 2nd, 3rd Purser; (Hotel Director Secretary); Front Desk Assistants; Computer Technicians; Information system Manager; Printer, Concierge.

HOTEL DIRECTOR

The Hotel Director is responsible for the management of the entire crew onboard with the exception of the bridge, deck, engineering departments and all other departments supervised by this department.

The department is the nerve center of the ship and handles all departmental administration procedures, duties include the implementation of all shipboard systems and services including schedules, inspections, training and communication budget management, he / she reports directly to the Vice President of Hotel Operations at the Head Office.

ASSISTANT HOTEL MANAGER

Is responsible for the various day to day operations onboard as directed by the Hotel Manager including trainings, inspections with the Hotel Manager and crew, must had previous hotel experience and a degree in hotel and restaurant management.

HOTEL CONTROLLER

Is the accountant controller onboard the ship, he /she is responsible for auditing and accounting procedures of everything from cash flow to ship supplies and inventories as directed by the Hotel Manager, duties include training and management accounting staff.

Degree in accounting, finance and/ or business required, computer skills, management experience essential.

Under His / Her control there is a team of auditors.

CHIEF PURSER

Is the business manager, responsible for the crew and passenger accounts, payroll, information services, the Printer's shop, purchase requisitions, shipboard concessions, communication with Customs and Immigration Officers in all ports and all complaint's.

The Purser's department also acts as the ship's bank, taking deposits from the ship's bars and retail outlets, exchanging currency for passengers, the retaining of passports for immigration purposes and safe keeping of valuables, the ship's daily newspaper is normally published adjacent to the office, the Editor assembles the next day schedule of activities, informative stories about the ship and upcoming ports and a round up of world news assisted by the translator for the various different nationalities aboard, the finished copy is taken to the Printer for publication, previous hotel experience preferable, a degree in hotel and restaurant management is require.

2ND, 3 RD PURSER, ASSISTANT PURSER, JUNIOR ASSISTANT PURSER, FRONT DESK ASSISTANTS, PA'S, GUEST SERVICES CO ORDINATOR, PRINTER, SECRETARIES

GENERAL INFORMATION

The above staff implement the companies policies and procedures to the passengers, accommodation change requests and problems, money transactions, communication between all departments, ships board announcements, etc.

The Pursers department Is the nerve center of the ship, providing information for both passengers and crew, the information/ desk reception is one of the first areas in which passengers seek services, therefore it is vital that staff are prepared to provide the required service s at all times, the duties of the front desk assistants vary depending on the ship, its itineraries and policies, in order to provide information requested it is their responsibility to familiarize themselves with the ship's layout, its history, entertainment for passengers, ship's service, ports of call, customs and immigrations, group functions and many other areas, many questions can be answered by reviewing the Cruise News, the ship listing of activities and services for passengers and crew.

CREW PURSER

Handles all documentation for the crew signing on and signing off, he/ she is responsible for maintaining passports of all crew, checking appropriates visa or work permits and handling all immigration and customs for the crew, he/ she orders, receives and distributes airline tickets for departing crew for vacation, transfer, medical, etc and any eventuality that may arise.

CONCIERGE

Reports directly to the Hotel Manager, he/ she should have a service minded attitude and is responsible for providing VIP service to all passengers occupying suites and on the VIP list, he/ she is also responsible for handling all requests for private cocktail parties and functions for passengers, obtaining tickets for special shows, making sure they are escorted on the tenders to shore, organizing bridge and galley tours, etc or simply obtaining items that passengers cannot find themselves.

COMPUTER TECHINICIAN / INFORMATION SYSTEM MANAGER

This position is increasingly in demand, he/ she is responsible for the supply and maintenance of all onboard software, a degree or certificated diploma is required with PC and Microsoft based systems or 4 years equivalent work experience, must be proficient in Windows 3.1, Windows 98 with Windows NT/Novell, UNIX and Ethernet and varying cabling topologies modifying date and training shipboard personnel.

CRUISE STAFF AND ENTERTAINMENT DEPARTMENT

The Cruise Director is responsible for the Cruise Staff and Entertainment departments, the Cruise Staff are responsible running all the day to day passengers activities, entertainment, shows, games, lectures, fitness, etc, they along with the Entertainment Staff are the most highly visible members of the crew onboard so it's SHOW TIME every time they leave their cabin and some Cruise Staff members are even double as entertainers, there are generally, they are generally two shows per evening which are Broadway type shows such as Cats, Grease, Stralight, Express, etc, along with performances from jugglers, magicians, ventriloquists, illusionists, piano players, duos, trios and quarters, etc.

CRUISE STAFF DEPARTMENT

Assistant Cruise Director, Administration Assistant, Aerobics Instructors, Art Auctioneers, Assistant Shore Excursion Manager, Disc Jockey, Fitness instructor, Gentleman dance Host, International Hosts, Hostesses, Port Lecture, Shore Excursion / Tour Manager, Sports Director, Television Technicians, Videographers, Water Sports / Dive Instructor, Youth Activities Co- coordinator

ENTERTAINMENT DEPARTMENT

Art Auctioneers, Assistant Stage Managers, Dancers, Entertainers, Lounge Performers, Musicians, Production Managers, Singers, Sound& Light Technicians, Stage Managers, Video Technicians

The Cruise Director is also responsible for instructors of varying types and below we have listed a small number of different topics covered:

Arts& Crafts, Astrology, Bridge, Backgammon, Golf, Handwriting Analysis, Numerology, Ballroom / Line Dancing, Psychic.

THE CRUISE DIRECTOR

The Cruise Director is the most prominent person onboard after the Captain, from a passenger point of view, once the ship is sailing it falls on this person shoulders to make the vacation is truly memorable event. He / She is responsible for all entertainment and recreation, he / she is the Master of Ceremonies at all shipboard functions, the personality of Cruise Director usually as a professional entertainment background and as the ability to make the public peaking, delegation and possess good organizational abilities, strong personality and diplomatic skills essential, management of cruise staff and is able to communicate well with officers, crew, passengers.

DEPUTY CRUISE DIRECTOR

He/ She is the Cruise Director thigh hand person sharing the workload of programming events and overseeing the smooth running of the department together with the co ordination of Cruise Staff personnel activity schedules, manages the day to day operation of activities and involves passengers, reports directly to the Cruise Director.

FITNESS DIRECTOR

He / She co ordinates and creates a comprehensive health and fitness program me for different levels of passengers, conducts aerobics, fitness, aqua aerobics and special health related classes, updates fitness industry standards for all exercise program me, maintains inventory of all exercise equipment, reporting daily any maintenance or repair problems and is responsible for all the cleanliness and safety precautions of gym and health club facilities, it helps if you are extrovert, a quick and critical thinker, witty, personable and articulate, you must also be service oriented and have the ability to take direction, must have previous experience or degree in sports, science or physical education.

INTERNATIONAL HOST/ HOSTESS

The International Host/ Hostess acts as a liaison with foreign speaking passengers ensuring that non English speaking passengers are part of any activity, must therefore have complete fluency in three to five languages-English, Italian, Spanish, German, French or even Portuguese, he/ she translates daily programs and gives public address announcements can be called upon to translate anything at any, assists in lifeboat drills and accompanies passengers on escort tours, reports directly to the Cruise Director, must have 1 or 2 years hotel or leisure experience and be able to read and write fluently in 3-5 languages as above mentioned, strong personality and social skills required.

PORT LECTURE

Prior to arrival in any port lecture gives a talk about the history of the city or country, this is followed by a explanation of the places of interest, he/ she must create a sheet of information for the port of call, this should be consistent with lecture material which is done in conjunction with the shore excursion Manager and local port tour agent, must have information about the port of call and advise passengers accordingly and assist shore excursion department in tour transportation and escort tours, he/ she is highly visible and accessible to passengers and also assists in lifeboat drills and accompanies passengers on escorted tours, must have travel related experience, strong personality and social skills required.

SHORE EXCURSION & TOUR MANAGERS

The Shore Excursion and Tour Manager is primary responsible for the presentation, supervision and arrangement of shore excursions offered in the various ports of call by the company, the department normally acts independently of other departments on the ships as it co ordinates with shore side personnel, he/she presents shore excursion, talks and slide presentations, communicates with port officials and participates in activities, escort tours and other duties directed by the Cruise Director, he/ she is accomplished in the awareness of the budget goals and along with the effective management, planning, implementation and monitoring of the entire onboard shore excursion program me, he/ she is highly visible and accessible to the passengers and also assists in lifeboat drills, reports directly to the Cruise Director or Hotel Manager, must have tourism or travel related experience, strong personality and social skills are required.

ART AUCTIONEERS

This is relatively a new position aboard the cruise ships and a excellent way for the company to create extra revenues, the pieces of art are displayed throughout the ships during the voyage giving the passengers a idea of what is for sale, the Auctioneers must have sales and public speaking experience and duties include conducting all art auctions, preparation for auctions and sales, transport viewing and storage, conduct daily viewing of art for the guests on the ship, conduct lecture describing the art being offered, serve as a Host during viewing frames during auctions and other times of the voyage, create and maintain accurate records, reporting, administration, etc, co coordinate delivery, packaging and labeling of all art at disembarkation, report all sold art to the ship's authorities plus any other duties that may be required to assist him.

DANCERS

There are many opportunities for singers/ dancers on the cruise ships, they are normally part of the production shows that are contracted by a cruise line trough entertainment agencies although some of the major companies to employ their own entertainment staff which most of them are listed in my NAUTICAL JOBS HUNTER 2 BOOK and in BELINDA KING PRODUCTIONS web site IN UK, which I know personally since many years ago, he/ she reports directly to the Cruise Director, he/ she must have experience in Broadway or musical theatre styles, must have strong stamina, personality and the ability to perform two shows a night seven days a week.

DISC JOCKEYS

DJ's must have a minimum of two to three years experience working in the Capacity of a Disc jockey in various entertainment situations, experience in serving a

Master of Ceremonies, must also have knowledge of current to dance music, familiarity with popular favorites from the past and ability to to mix for dancing, a DJ should be extroverted, quick and critical thinker, witty, personable and articulate, must be service oriented and have the ability to take direction, he/ she is responsible for setting the appropriate atmosphere through the use of pre record music for any assigned activities with the specific responsibility for the night club, maintenance, storage and inventory of all musical equipment and supplies, must have entertainment and musical background in recreation, hotel or nightclub.

Strong personality and social skills required.

ENTERTAINERS

Feature performers come onboard for a short period (usually under 1 Month) and perform a completely self contained show providing their Own music and materials, they generally perform 1-2 shows per cruise, They are treated as passengers, but report directly to the Cruise Director

GENTLEMAN HOST

Must be over the age of 45 and preferably single, smart, articulate, Physically fit, good conversationalist, good listener and most important, a Good ballroom dancer, gentleman hosts are in great demand because of the increasing growing number of ladies who cruise without partners, they are specially recruited to provide dance and social partners for lady passengers, they also host a table in the dining room, act as partners at cocktail parties, dance classes and accompany ladies in shore excursions.

Typical benefits would be:

Return air ticket, single or shared stateroom, a drink allowance, all services of the ship provided to paying passengers, shore excursions, there is normally no salary for this position, great tips yes.

GUEST LECTURES

This can be a fun job if you have special skills or hobbies, there is not usually a salary for this position, you do however get a cruise for yourself and companion in return for just a few hours of your time.

There is no age limit and you can be asked to join another ship in the fleet several times a year, the most common subjects are arts and crafts, Bridge, Numerology, Fortune telling.

Hand writing, analysis, golf, instruction, antiques and self improvement, but there are many other areas for lecturing in if you have the knowledge, typical benefits would be:

Return airline ticket, short term cruise, free single or shared stateroom, a drink allowance, all services of the ship provided to paying passengers, shore excursions, dining with passengers and / or officer's mess, if salaried is between 600 to 1000 pounds per month.

LOUNGE PERFORMER

Lounge performers entertain in certain locations such as piano bars, cafes, nightclubs, providing their own music and materials,

They must have the ability to perform several hours a night at least six days a week is essential.

PRODUCTION MANAGER

Production managers oversee the production shows and are responsible for the smooth transition of a new production cast from on shore to onboard the ship's, he/ she directs and manage all rehearsals on shore and onboard, must have a strong musical theatre background and/ or experience in a Broadway show type of productions.

STATE MANAGER

Responsible for running the production shows and managing the technical staff, also assists at any of the passenger activities which are require technical assistance, reports directly to the Cruise Director, must have extensive technical and practical experience including state of the art computerized sound mixing boards.

TELEVISION TECHNICIAN / VIDEOGRAPHER

Should have a minimum of one or two years experience in television production with specific technical experience in editing, camera operation and behind the scenes detail, a extroverted, quick and critical thinker, personable and articulate, must also have the ability to give direction to other entertainer/ staff members in the preparation and execution of entertainment presentations, he/ she is responsible for the maintaining of onboard television network, passenger and crew news, satellite news services, videotaping, movie schedules, maintenance of equipment and passenger activities, must have a highly technical background and educational in film, video and television production, knowledge of computer and electronic state of the art equipment is necessary.

WATER SPORTS / DIVE INSTRUTORS

Instructors conduct the snorkeling and give program me, maintain dive boats equipment and are responsible for the health and safety of the passengers, they also are involved with some of the no water related activities as instructed by the assistant cruise director, must have a dive instructor certificate and have worked at instructor level with a report or dive operation, the national association of communication, organizational and sale skills, computer literacy, ability to control inventory and quality knowledge of marine life and marine ecology, must have a extroverted, friendly personality and is responsible for the entire implementation of the program me from sale to taking professional format, must monitor all sales and revenue to ensure that the program me meets and adheres to budget goals.

BAR DEPARTMENT

The Bar department is responsible for serving alcoholic beverages in areas such as the casinos, nightclubs, disco, decks, restaurants, room service, private parties and all bars and bar areas.

The Bar Manager is responsible for the following staff:

Assistant Bar Manager, Bar supervisor, Bar Waiter/ Waitress, Bartender, Bar Utility, Bar accountant

BAR MANAGER / ASSISTANT BAR MANAGER / BAR SUPERVISOR

Supervises the entire operation of the bar department, oversees training and management of the bar staff cleanliness of lounges, reports directly to the Hotel Manager, must have a minimum three to five year food& beverage experience preferably having been trained in the entire bar department operations

BARWAITER / WAITRESS

Responsible for serving alcohol beverages and others to, passengers in all bar areas, lounges, casino, restaurant, set up bar stations, assist in the stocking and cleaning, must have experience working in restaurants and hotels.

BARTENDER

Responsible for serving drinks to passengers in lounges and decks, bar, set up, cleaning and stocking, he/ she follows inventory control procedures and is responsible for maintenance, where is possible for training and instructions to new staff, especially international.

BEAUTY SALON

The Salon will offer a wide range of beauty related services such as hairdressing, manicures, pedicures, massages, etc, the Salon Manager is responsible for the following personnel in his department: Assistant Managers, Masseuse/Masseur, Hairdressers, Hairstylist, Barbers.

SALON MANAGER

The Salon Manager oversees entire operations of the beauty salon, accounting and

Management of Salon staff, reports directly to the Hotel Manager, must have two/three years experience in a beauty salon and be a graduate and have certification from a accredited beauty salon academy, managerial experience and public speaking skills required for passengers.

ASSISTANT MANAGER

He/ She manages the day to day operations of the beauty salon as directed by the Salon Manager, responsible for salon staff schedules, reports directly to the Salon Manager, must have one to two years experience in a beauty salon, certification from a accredited beauty academy is necessary together with managerial experience.

BEAUTICIAN

Provides beauty related services to passengers, e.g, manicures, pedicures, facials, hair treatment, reports directly to the Salon Manager, must have one or two years of experience in a beauty salon and have been graduated from a beauty academy.

MASSEUR / MASSEURE

Provides massages to passengers and to crew members as the schedule allows at a reduce rate, reports directly to the Salon Manager, massage, therapists must be licensed and possess extensive knowledge of muscles and any other relevant medical terminology, must have one or two years experience as licensed professional masseuse.

SEE PORTRAIT OF STEINERS FOR GUIDELINES

A PORTRAIT OF STEINER

Steiner is the largest spa operator in the world, over the years they have gained more contacts to operate and sometimes to design spas onboard cruise ships, the nature of the beauty industry as rapidly changed and Steiner in keeping with the times as incorporated many of the latest thalasso therapy, hydrotherapy, and thermal treatments in the new spas, Mandara spa, another leading beauty concessionaire onboard the cruise ships is now part of the Steiner increasing their spas onboard above hundred cruise ships.

REQUIREMENTS

Care minded, service oriented lots of team spirit and energy, a sense of adventure and a love of people.

HAIRDRESSERS

Require to have completed a three year hairdressing apprenticeship at a full timer college, they must be fully qualified in both ladies and gentleman's hairdressing, successful applicants will require to do a trade test.

DINING ROOM WAITER / WAITRESS

Reports to the Head Waiter, he/ she is responsible for a station which normally comprises of approximately 24 passengers, his/ hear duties are to learn the passenger's names as their stations, serve them promptly in a friendly manner with the correct food ordered, known the menu well, explain the menu and suggest dishes to passengers who don't have idea what to order and to keep their work station to the highest standards, his/ her is in charge of the busboy (Runner), hours are long, 10 to 12 hours per day, but as new sea laws said at the current time most of the cruise liners are scheduling 11 hours per day, seven days a week, minimum of one to two years hotel or restaurant experience in related position is requested.

ASSISTANT WAITER/ WAITRESS

Responsible to set tables, serve passengers as directed by the Waiter, keep menus clean, clean tables between sittings, menu knowledge, minimum one or two years experience in hotel or restaurant related positions.

WINE STEWARD

Must be able to promote the wine sales and drinks, should possess a comprehensive knowledge of wines obtained by work experience or by a appropriate college course, he/ she serve wine at the correct temperature, needs to be knowledgeable of the wine list and be able to discuss and suggest personality, must have minimum of one or two years hotel or restaurant experience in related positions.

THE SHIP'S GALLEY-KITCHEN DEPARTMENT

This department is responsible for food planning, preparation and quality control of all meals served onboard the ship's, further responsibilities include food costs, storage, ordering, distribution and stock cost control of all food supplies, cleaning and maintenance of the galley and maintaining the highest possible food standards by the companies.

The Executive Chef is responsible for the entire team, for all Chefs, Sous Chefs, Pastry Chefs, Storekeepers, Butchers, Bakers, Ice Carvers, Cleaners and Dishwashers in this department, listed bellow are many of the varied position types, which make up this department.

Assistant Executive Chef, Sous Chef, Chef Tournant, 1st Cook, 2nd Cook, 3rd Cook, Cook helper, Cook Trainee, Crew Cook, Crew Cook Trainer, Crew Cook utility, Cooks runners, Officer / Crew Mess Man, Provision Master / Storekeeper, Butcher Supervisor, Assistant Butcher Supervisor, Butcher, Butcher Helper, Butcher Trainee, Butcher utility, Pastry Chef Supervisor, Chef de Partie,, 1st Pastry man, 2nd Pastry man, Pastry Cook, Pastry helper, Pastry Trainee, Baker Supervisor, Assistant Baker Supervisor,1st Baker, 2nd Baker, 3rd Baker, Baker Helper, Galley Cleaner, Utility Cleaner, Pantry Man, Head Buffet Man, Buffet Runner, Coffee Man, Dishwasher (KP), Pot washer, Head Day cleaner, Day Utility, Head Night cleaner, Night Cleaner, Night Utility, Crew Cleaner, Ice Carver.

EXECUTIVE CHEF

Reports directly to the Hotel Manager and is in charge of the running of the kitchen, nowadays the Executive chef role is largely administrative with the constant planning that is required, he is responsible for a large team of Chefs who do all the food preparations, quality control, stock control, cost control of all food supplies, cleaning and maintenance of galley and maintains the highest possible food standards set by the companies, must have hotel and restaurant experience of no less than five years and be graduate from a accredited culinary school, USPH Certificates essential.

SOUS CHEF

Supervises assigned staff with certain food preparations as directed by the Executive Chef, food planning, preparation, quality control, cleaning and maintenance of galley and maintains the highest possible food standards set by the companies, must have four to five years experience in hotel or restaurant and be graduate from a accredited culinary school. USPH certificate essential.

1St COOK

Supervises 2nd and 3rd cooks, bakers, pastry cooks, cleaners and provisions, food preparation and cooking responsibilities as directed by the Executive Chef and maintains highest possible food standards set by the companies, should have two or three years experience in a hotel or restaurant. Graduate from a accredited culinary school.

2ND AND 3RD COOK

Responsible for food preparations and cooking as directed by the 1st Cook, supervision of bakers, pastry cooks, cleaners and provisions, must have two years experience in hotel or restaurant.

CHEF DE PARTIE

Responsible for the supervision of a section, either pastry, larder, sauce, etc, oversee the developing creating and preparing food in their department, maintain high standards as set by the companies, supervises cleaning and maintenance of assigned areas, culinary background of no less than three years in a hotel or restaurant experience or prior experience on board required.

COMMIS CHEF

Preparation and cooking of food as directed by the 1st Cook, must have at least 2 years prior hotel or restaurant experience.

PROVISION STOREMAN

Responsible for the entire storage, distribution and stocks cost control of all food supplies as directed by the Executive Chef, food& beverage background is essential, knowledge of accounting and cost control procedures, graduate from a accredited culinary school with emphasis on food and beverage operations preferable.

BUTCHER SUPERVISOR

Responsible for the supervising of all butcher staff in the proper handling, preparation, storage of meats, works closely with the Executive Chef regarding ordering, distribution and stock control of all meat supplies.

BUTCHER/ BUTCHER HELPER/ BUTCHER TRAINEE/ BUTCHER UTILITY

Butcher staff is responsible for the proper handling, preparation and storage of meats as directed by the Butcher Supervisor.

PASTRY CHEF SUPERVISOR

Responsible for the supervision of the pastry staff, overseeing the developing, creating and preparation of all pastries, maintains high standards as set by the company, supervises cleaning spaces and maintenance of assigned areas, must have a culinary background of no less than three years hotel or restaurant experience.

1SR AND 2ND PASTRYMAN

Responsible for creating and preparing all pastries as directed by the Pastry Chef supervisor, must have experience of no less than two years in hotel or restaurant.

BAKER SUPERVISOR

Responsible for the supervision of the bakery staff, oversees the preparation and cooking of all bakery products, supervises the cleaning and maintenance of assigned areas, must have at least three years hotel or restaurant experience.

1ST AND 2ND BAKER

All bakery staff are responsible for the preparation and cooking of bakery products as directed by the Bakery Supervisor.

HEAD BUFFET MAN

Responsible for the supervision of setting up and preparation of all buffets, assisting in serving passengers.

GALLEY ASSISTANTS

Are responsible for all general cleaning and preparation duties and dish washing machines, in most cruise ships over 20.000 meals are prepared daily and over 40.000 glasses are washed, no experience necessary.

PANTRY MAN

Responsible for the maintenance and cleaning of pantry areas as directed by the Executive Chef, no experience necessary.

CLEANERS

Responsible for the day and night cleaning for the entire galley kitchens, refrigerators, storage areas, etc, no experience necessary.

BUFFET RUNNER / COFFEE MAN

Responsible for the setting up, cleaning of all buffet areas and equipment as directed by the Head Buffet Man, no experience necessary

GIFT SHOP DEPARTMENT / RETAIL DEPARTMENT

Cruise ships have arcades of shops onboard offering a wide selection of goods, the stores offer items with the ships logo, souvenirs, designer clothes, jewelry, perfumes, snacks and sundries, etc, the Gift Shop Manager is responsible for the following personnel:

GIFT SHOP MANAGER, ASSISTANT GIFT SHOP MANAGER, SALES STAFF

Gift shop manager oversee entire gift shop operations and manage retail staff, must have three years to five years experience in retail, managerial experience necessary and public speaking skills for onboard demonstrations.

ASSISTANT GIFT SHOP MANAGER

Oversees the day to day operations and assists in managing the retail staff, reports directly to the Gift Shop

Manager, one to two years retail management experience is necessary together with public speaking skills.

SALES ASSISTANT

Reports to Gift Shop Manager

High school diploma or equivalent, two to four years experience of previous retail merchandising, display and sales experience is required, ability to perform arithmetic operations involving monetary units and calculating ratios and percentages, ability to operate key adding machine, counter and alphabetical keyboard basic clerical speed and accuracy skills are necessary, must able to speak English, read and write, speak clearly, distinctly and cordially with costumers, additional language is a plus.

Able to carry up to 50 pounds, the position involves standing for up 12 hours per day in some companies, Responsible for selling merchandise onboard gift shops, the minimum amount of hours worked per week is 56.

Stock shelves, counters or tables with merchandise, set up advertising displays, table sales and daily promotions, ticket merchandise and price correctly, use cash register to total customers purchases and determine bill, accept credit card payments through point of sales, wrap or bag merchandises for costumers, organize storeroom, keep records of sales, prepare inventories in shop and storeroom

HOUSEKEEPING DEPARTMENT

Chief Steward / Housekeeper, Assistant Chief Steward / Housekeeper, Floor Supervisor, Head Room steward / stewardess, Cabin Steward / Stewardess, Assistant Steward

/ Stewardess, Bellboy, Cleaner / Utility Cleaner, Laundry supervisor, Assistant Laundry supervisor, Laundry keeper, Pool Attendant, Bell Captain, Butler.

CHIEF STEWARD / HOUSEKEEPER

Is responsible to supervise the housekeeping department, reports directly to the Hotel Manager, duties include managing staff, cleanliness of all passenger cabins, public areas with the exception of the dining room, offices and crew areas, the maintenance of inventories, requisitions and care of equipment, the supervision of cabin services, room service, bar service and bell service, the handling of baggage and distribution to and from cabins at the beginning and end of the cruises, must have three to five years experience in hotels or resorts and have a hotel management degree.

CABIN STEWARD / STEWARDESS

Cleans and maintain passenger cabins and verandas, change bed linen and towels, bathmats, etc, makes up beds for the day and turn them down at night.

Ensures a adequate supply of items such as soap, tissues, toilet paper matches are maintained, provides ice and fruit on a daily basis (more if requested)

Room service as requested and bar items as requested, distribute and display company literature and notices.

Removes waste items and dispose of a central locations, takes and return laundry7 dry cleaning as per guest requests, help guests with cabin fittings and facilities with particular reference to air conditioning and television/ telex, assists in embarkation, meeting and directing guests, ensure all used items of crockery and glass are removed from cabin and washed and stored in the pantry, assists in maintaining the pantry to a United States Public Health Standard (AUPH), spring cleans and have ready for inspection designated cabins as required, ensures all maid's carts, trolleys, etc are frequently cleaned and removed from passenger always and properly stowed after use, assist in maintaining the cleanliness of passenger alleyways.

ASSISTANT CABIN STEWARD / STEWARDESS

Assists the cabin steward / stewardess with the daily duties.

BUTLER

In many of the more expensive luxury ships there are butlers to pander to the requests of the passengers in the penthouse suites, appropriate training and / or experience is essential for such work, although the hours are long, gratuities are generally excellent

WAITER / WAITRESS

A diploma from a recognized apprenticeship program me or equivalent, qualifications and experience at least two years full time restaurant service experience in a 5 star hotel or Michelin star restaurant is required, he/ she is responsible for a station onboard and for his assistant waiter/ waitress, responsible to explain the daily menus and to recommend as well, responsible to check the set up tables, if nothing is missing, to check the cleanness of the menus and items, crockery, cutlery, glasses, table cloths, napkins, salt / pepper, sugar bowls, salt / pepper, Tabasco, Worcester Sauce, Horseradish sauce, parmesan cheese, saucers, coffee cups, bread crumbier, chairs, tables, flower arrange, responsible to direct the assistant waiter when they are providing meals to the passengers, in my opinion I recommend them to study each other them qualities and skills so that they can provide a better service with signals in a professional manner.

ASSISTANT WAITER / WAITRESS

A diploma from a recognized apprenticeship program me or equivalent, one year experience working previously in a good quality hotel / restaurant .

WINE WAITER / WAITRESS

Two years experience in a 5 star hotel / restaurant operations, applicants need to include in any resume any diploma or certificate of basic or wine / beverage course and/ or seminar attended, applications should not have only book knowledge but should be able to prove themselves as a sales person.

MEDICAL DEPARTMENT

MEDICAL STAFF

On a ship is usually a fully equipment hospital, a pharmacy, x ray room and a small operating theatre, medical problems of all descriptions arise from heart attacks to kidney stones, workplace accidents and sadly sometimes death.

Minor surgery can be performed but every effort is made to stabilize the patient until a shore based hospital is reached, for this reason a trauma and emergency background is essential for applicants.

Passengers may arrive with instructions from their personal doctors for treatment and medication and each port presents its own special brands of illness, for example in some countries it is not safe to drink the water or have drinks with ice cubes, there is sea sickness, bruised or broken limbs and even babies delivered, so all in all medical side of the business is a very busy one.

Doctor's employed by large cruise companies are generally licensed in Canada, Great Britain or the U.S, they are given senior officer status together with the appropriate salary and conditions, part of Doctor's duties is supporting the Captain and Security Officer in the investigation of any accident involving passengers have to be investigated in case they become the subject of a insurance claim and together with accidents involving crew members, have to be entered in the Captain's Log which in turn as to be supported by evidence from the Doctor, experience RGN Nurses or equivalent, preferably with accident & emergency trauma care or intensive care experience, assist Doctor, Nurses are also given officer status (Two Stripes)

Doctors are also assisted in the case of heart attacks by dive instructions experienced in CPR, there also opportunities for Medical orderlies with the appropriate experience, on some of the bigger ships there are also Dentists onboard

DOCTORS

Must be licensed physicians, state board certified, graduate from a accredited medical school and have drug enforcement administration (DEA) certificate, experience with cardiac and primary care, trauma, internal, family and emergency medicine, some doctors prefer to cruise free for services rendered, this is offered a 2-4 weeks cruise free but companies will require doctor's schedule well in advance before considering a candidate for this position Must be graduate from a accredited nursing school with a minimum of three years recent hospital experience, experience necessary with cardiac care emergency and internal medicine, must have a advanced life support certificate or equivalent.

MEDICAL ORDERLINES

Medical orderliness with appropriate training and experience are also employed in most ships depending on the size, they usually have Pretty officer status.

DENTISTS

Positions for Dentists are usually only available on extended cruises such as world cruises, he/ she is responsible for the treatment of passengers and crew.

PHOTOGRAPHY DEPARTMENT

The photographers are some of the busiest people onboard the ships and everywhere during the voyage, they can be found at the gangway when the guests are boarding ship, at formal nights such as cocktail party, Captain's dinner table, in fact anywhere a party is taking place, photographers have to be snapped and process against the clock, applicants should possess a high standard of photography skills together with practical ability and experience in printing developing, dark room work, together with the sale of photos is often a large part of the job, salaries can be very good in this area

In this department there's a Photo Manager, a Assistant Photo Manager and a Photographer, the Photo Manager reports directly to the Hotel Manager.

RESTAURANT SERVICE SINS

1. Not acknowledging guests with eye contact and a smile within 30 seconds.
2. Not thanking the guests as they leave. Last impression.
3. Not remembering the guests likes and dislikes.
4. Not opening the front door for guests.
5. Silverware set askew on the tables.
6. Table top that isn't picture perfect.
7. Forks with bent tines.
8. Unevenly folded napkins.
9. Chipped glassware.
10. Tables not completely set when guests being seated.
11. Dead or wilted flowers on the tables.
12. Tables that are not level.
13. Salt and pepper shakers that are empty.
14. Salt or sugar crusted inside the shakers.
15. Carelessly placed items on the tables.
16. Table linen with small holes, rips or burns.

17. Clutter or junk. Watch the trays, dumb waiters (small tables) etc.
18. Pictures on the wall not revealed.
19. Tables not properly cleared.
20. Burned out light bulbs.
21. Clattering dishes. Be quiet.
22. Dropping china, silverware or glassware.
23. Murky or smelly water in flower vases.
24. Wobbly tables or chairs.
25. Broken chairs.
26. Needing to be centre of attention. Give the ego a break.
27. An "I'm doing you a favor" attitude.
28. Socializing with certain guests while ignoring others.
29. Being too familiar or excessively chatty.
30. Having a visible reaction to the amount of the tip.
31. Ignoring obvious attempts to get attention.
32. Making light of a guest's complaint.
33. No sense of humor.
34. Orders that arrive incomplete.
35. Not acknowledging guests as soon as they are seated.
36. Not providing service to tables in order of their arrival.
37. Wrong pacing: meal service too fast or too slow.
38. Not providing a place for meal debris-e.g., shells.
39. Food sitting visible on dumb waiters (small table).
40. Necessary condiments that don't arrive with food.
41. Lack of eye contact.
42. Talking to the order pad.
43. Not repeating each item as the guest orders.
44. Not naming each item as you serve.
45. Addressing the woman as "the lady" (times are changing).

46. Thumbs on the plate during service.
47. Stacking or scraping dishes in front of the guests.
48. Approaching a table with another dirty dishes.
49. Entering the guest conversation without invitation.
50. Interrupting or asking questions while a guest mouth is full.
51. Handling silverware by the eating surfaces.
52. Holding glasses by bow or rim.
53. Language that is too formal or casual.
54. Asking men for their orders before asking woman.
55. Not having total focus when at the table.
56. Giving guests the feeling of being "processed".
57. Not really listening when spoken to.
58. Being too hurried to be attentive.
59. Not establishing rapport with the guests.
60. Appearing stressed or out of control.
61. Not bringing something the guest request.
62. Providing inconsistent service (Dig down, you can do it).
63. Not bringing a replacement (sugar, butter, etc).
64. Not removing extra place settings.
65. Inability to answer basic menu questions. (Pay attention to the before meal meetings, what you don't known, ask).
66. Not knowing what brands are carried at the bar.
67. Placing a cocktail napkin askew or upside down.
68. Not warning about hot plates or beverages.
69. Dropping plates instead of presenting them.
70. Not brining all the service ware needed for the menu item.
71. Serving with an elbow in the guest's face.
72. Inconsistent service methods.

73. Not refilling water, coffee or other beverages such as wine.
74. Not moving with the "speed of the room".
75. Not checking back within a few minutes of service the course.
76. Not visually checking on each table regularly.
77. Not clearing one course completely before serving the next (e.g. toast, finger bowls.)
78. Remove plates before all guests are finished.
79. Clearing plates without permission.
80. Not clearing plates properly.
81. Vanishing waiters.
82. Not continuing to service the table once you have presented the check.
83. Watching while the guest completes the credit card slip.
84. Dribbling wine on the table while pouring.
85. Resting the wine bottle on the rim of the glass.
86. Spilling food and beverage.
87. Wet, stained or incorrectly added checks.
88. Poor personal sanitation practices (touching, scratching, etc.).
89. Standing around without doing nothing.
90. Using poor grammar addressing a guest.
91. Pointing in the dining room.
92. Rating pocket change.
93. Walking past items dropped on the floor.
94. Answering a question with a question.
95. Soiled or ill fitting uniforms.
96. Filthy footwear.
97. Slouching or poor posture.

98. Distracting accessories (such as mobiles-never take your mobile on service, that's nothing professional and they are a source of problems between colleagues).
99. Obvious hangovers.
100. Bandages on hand.
101. Smelling like cigarettes.
102. Excuses for anything-anytime.
103. Personal conversations loud enough for guests to hear.
104. Whining or complaining.
105. Arguments or display anger.
106. Flirting with guests.
107. Speaking in incomplete sentences.
108. Not serving hot food, hot.
109. Cold bread or rolls stale around the edges.
110. Incomplete orders.
111. Improperly chilled wine or beer.
112. Drinks without a stirrer or straw.
113. Improper glass ware.
114. Dried out or slimy fruit garnish.
115. Lukewarm coffee.
116. Overly strong or weak ice tea.
117. No fresh glasses with a fresh drink.
118. Water, ice tea or coffee not properly refilled.
119. Coffee in the saucer.
120. Pouring anything from a stained container.
121. Awkward, improper or inept wine service.
122. Popping a champagne cork.
123. Pouring regular coffee into a cup instead of decaf.
124. Not getting the order right the first time. (takes practice).
125. Serving the wrong drink.

126. Not serving wine promptly.
127. Dirty or spotted flat ware.
128. Crumbs on chairs.
129. Meetings between colleagues while on service, when others are working, doing something,(cannot happen)
130. Bad faces while on service.
131. When on service – As a Waiter / Waitress, if you are inside the dining room and need to collect any meals in the kitchen what you can do on the way? If you are a truly professional, you should take any dirty glasses, cutlery, plates, etc inside to the kitchen porter on your way, this is the best procedure to do not waste time if you want to finish earlier.

STATUS OF CRUISE STAFF

This is general and does not apply on all cruise liners as the job description can be different

FOURS STRIPES

Captain; Chief Engineer, Hotel Manager, Staff Captain, Staff Chief engineer

THREE STRIPES

Assistant Hotel Manager, Chief electrician, Chief Officer,, Chief Radio (Communication officer), Cruise Director, Executive Chef, Food &Beverage Manager, Ship's Doctor, Purser

TWO and HALF STRIPES

Assistant Food & Beverage Manager, Assistant (Hotel& Crew) Purser

Bar Manager, Chief Security Officer, Chief Steward,, 1st Officer (Deck & Engineering etc), Housekeeper.

TWO STRIPES

Nurse, 2nd Officer (Deck & Engineering, etc), 2nd Purser, 1st Manager

ONE and HALF STRIPES

Senior Secretary,, 3rd Officer (Deck& Engineering, etc) 3rd Purser

ONE STRIPES

Cadet, 4th Officer, (Deck& Engineering, etc), 4th Purser, Petty Officer

Please note that staff members in managerial positions such as beauty salon managers, chefs, maitre d hotels, shop, casino and senior social staff may have officer status and privileges.